Night Road to Life

Ferdinando Manzo

Night Road to Life
Ferdinando Manzo

First edition 2016 published by Sydney School of Arts & Humanities
15-17 Argyle Place, Millers Point, NSW 2000, Australia

www.ssoa.com.au

ISBN: 978-0-9945441-3-1

Poems Copyright
© Ferdinando Manzo 2016

All rights reserved. Without limiting the rights under copyright reserved above, no part of this publication may be reproduced, stored in or introduced into a retrieval system, or transmitted, in any form or by any means (electronic, mechanical, photocopying, recording or otherwise), without the prior written permission of both the copyright owner and the publisher. Any unauthorised act in relation to this publication may be liable to legal prosecution. Email: enquiry@ssoa.com.au

Cover picture: Ferdinando Manzo
Cover design: Ferdinando Manzo

Dedication

To my Nonna Titina, hope to see you on the next road life in *Dawn of a day with no name*

To my little niece Ada, wishing her one shining road in life without *Regrets of yesterday* or *Fear of tomorrow*

Acknowledgements

Thanks to Mum and Dad for letting me live my road life.

To Mariella Parmendola, who assists me anytime, everywhere.

To Melina Marquez, for her time after work sharing a beer with me and helping with my poems.

Author biography

Ferdinando Manzo is a professional journalist, born in Torre del Greco in the province of Napoli. He worked as an editor for Metropolis Network for about fifteen years, also collaborating as assistant producer to the production of Metropolis TV programs. He now lives in Australia where he works as a freelance reporter and author. *L'uomo che salvò il mondo* is his first novel, published in Italian by Lettere Animate Editore. His first short story in English is *Arco, the legend of the blue vortex*, published by Sydney School of Arts & Humanities.

Contents

Foreword	10
A melancholy path	13
Ruins	14
An attempt	15
The hookah witch	16
A choice	17
Those nights	18
A night flight	19
Dawn of a day with no name	20
Gateway to a child's world	22
Regrets of yesterday	23
Fear of tomorrow	24
Today	25
The butterfly and the spider	26
A lapse of memory	27
Song in the game of souls	28
Hyde Park dreaming	30
Nessy	31
Ghosts and gun	32
A seagull	33
You in a thought	34
The sea of love	35
The forgotten beach	36
Lost in the abyss	37
The oblivion of the forgotten	38
The voice of the universe	39
The missing moon	40
Jupiter and Venus	41
Andromeda's revenge	42
Chaos	43
Eclipse	44
Supernova	45
A night in a glass	46

The silence of the wind	47
A dark pub	48
A glass fixation	50
Unforgettable obsession	51
The last rose	52
Red lanterns	53
Lights in the night	54
Venus's eyes	56
I would tell you that	57
The sky above us	58
Waiting for the rain	60
Me and you	61
Night road to life	62

Foreword

Ferdinando Manzo arrived out of the wide blue yonder. Having had his first novel published in Italy by a major publisher last year, he was here in Sydney looking for a space to continue his writing.

He found a niche, deskspace at Sydney School of Arts & Humanities, and within a short time produced a short story in tandem with the subject of his fantasy novel, a story of the sea. The tale was called *ARCO: the legend of the blue vortex*. It was well-received.

He'd turned from journalism to creative writing along with his move from Italy to Australia. Now comes a book of poetry, which causes me to wonder at his agility in crossing genres to produce such original creative writing intricacies.

Certainly, themes of the sea and the emotions, particularly the deeply felt joys and melancholies experienced by men, are a touchstone of his work.

In *The hookah witch* the poet concludes, 'I search for a dream already disappeared'. *The sea of love* finds him 'chasing the dream that retreats in the backwash of another life'. In *Hyde Park dreaming* the spectacle is intriguing but ends abruptly once there's a recognition that his 'other' isn't there. A later poem, *Lost in the abyss,* describes how 'ghosts circle like drunks on a ship in a stormy sea'.

And where emotions flow, drink follows closely behind so that *A glass fixation* is also a suitable subject for

contemplation 'constricted in a bottle half full on the bar'.
But Manzo's thoughts are not bound to fluidity; they fly to the greatest heights of exhilaration in poems such as, *The sky above us*, which displays 'a mantle of stars that burns in my heart' and in the evocative lines of *Eclipse*: 'the moon rose, bright between the eyelids of the night'. Even the constellation Andromeda is given due recognition, breaking her chains and ready for revenge, before another poem *The voice of the universe* explores 'a hidden legend as far away as waves in outer space'.

A distinctive quality of this collection of poems is its musicality – the sounds of words carefully chosen, and their rhythms. The pleasing effect of the sensuality of sounds, ranging from gentleness to the drama of sex, is in tune with the gamut of human emotion. Perhaps Manzo's skill in tapping into harmonious resonance arises in the visceral qualities the poet gains from his capacity to draw on his mother tongue as well as his secondary language, English.

Whatever the source, Ferdinando Manzo has produced a resounding study of the senses that stays with the reader.

Christine Williams
Director, Sydney School of Arts & Humanities

A melancholy path

There is no other life
in the melancholy
of a finished season,
in a solitude made of smiles,
women, wine,
in which what you follow
is a false path
empty
as each day has betrayed you
dark
as the colours of life reduce to a pen's ink
trivial
as the sweetness that comes in your bed.
Back then,
you'd stop for a moment:
so fast, so subtle, so intense,
eternal.

Ruins

Romance in the twilight
of set aside feelings.
Ardour born out of revenge
that flows like a river
under a slab of ice.
Love consumed in wailing.

Passions are betrayed by thoughts
in a moment of pleasure,
seeking for a familiar moan
between forgotten sheets
of abandoned rooms,
sliding, distracted,
on the ruins of a love
in the memory of pain
in search of an illusion.

An attempt

I tried to understand
to look into the shadows
beyond emotions.
I tried to hear
that slow breath that smells of life
the one discordant note in a melody.
I tried to ford the injury
between currents of sloth
leading to despondent waves.
I experienced the emptiness of an hour
locked between the gold hands
of a diamond watch.
I tried everything —
and still I haven't grasped
the sudden, unique instant
so deep and rational
which leads to truth.
And madness.

The hookah witch

Through the eyes of a festive crowd
inebriated by artificial laughter
she was smoking a hookah of desire,
distilled vodka with sensuality,
while smoke pervaded the room,
thin clouds filled by desire.
In the anxiety consumed in watching her
the vision once found
vanished in the scent of what burns
between the filter and the paper,
a reality suspended
between today and tomorrow
between the possible and the impossible.
Along a ribbon of passion,
which lies in one night
among cars whizzing home
I search for a dream
already disappeared.

A choice

I was alone
mournful
with that sense of emptiness that takes me
on those nights you do not know,
no one knows,
when you would,
anyone would,
those nights that I need
someone or something.
You or a pub.
I thought of you, I watched you
in that picture never faded in thought.

I was embattled
between desire and pride
craving and laziness.
I thought of your house
of what I would find
if I came to you.
Your embrace
your kisses
your smile
your face
your lips
your eyes.

If I came I would find you
just you, only you.

At the pub, I could find
many replicas of you
and a few bottles.

So I decided …

Those nights

Those nights spent on street corners
watching the smoke from exhaust pipes mingle in the air
as incomplete ideas
fugitives thoughts
from the prison of a life
spent drifting
on a past road
riding remorse
playing with hours
without taste
devoid of passion
sunk in disappointment
devoured by the dullness
of a radio that plays
the sadness of a verse
the absurdity of a poem
the futility of the time
that's gone
following not fate
but agony.

A night flight

I would like to capture
the feeling of a night flight
between dreams and fears
anxiety and pleasure
in an unexpected sigh
for a newborn passion
in an embrace without obligation
timeless for a moment
in the smile of a stranger's face
that disappears in the morning
in a car that drives
desire to memory,
love to Utopia.

The dawn of a day with no name

In the dawn of a day with no name
I meet you again

to forget my pain
to capture the sense
of a kiss launched
in the solitude
of a dance where death spares deceit
in a chorus of voices
becoming more distant.

In the dawn of a day with no name
I meet you again

to feel still alive
the love of a smile
that fled as the last breath
from the limbo of a world in a room
opened to the sky,
returned to childhood,
to a smell of lacquer.

In the dawn of a day with no name
I meet you again

to wash from your face
the storm of memories
of tears weeping clouds
in the solitude of a park.

I miss you
I love you,
always that child holding your hand.

In the dawn of a day with no name
I meet you again

to hug and say goodbye:
ciao nonna.

The gateway to a child's world

(to my grandmother)

With you forever the door closes
on a childhood dragging its
dreams, fantasies.

With you forever the door closes
on the lightness of a child
who looked for adventures behind a sofa
who hunted mysteries in dishes on display never used
who found treasures of chocolate hidden in aged
furniture.

With you forever the door closes
on a child's discoveries
the first hand-written letters sent to a distant country
the craft workshop pinched within the walls of a room
a world of play that opened to a veranda.

With you forever the door closes
on a city, on the world of a child,
leaving pain and pleasure.

Regrets of yesterday

He believed he could see in the mirror
another face of himself
he could hear in a shell
the undertow of life
he could touch in a face
the sweetness of a smile
he could breathe from a leaf's sprout
the scent of infinity
he could find truth from
the study of the afterlife.
He believed he could
but he died without knowing.

Fear of Tomorrow

Walking on George Street
a scared man met a hobo
who was drinking wine
counting money, reading Hemingway.
With his open hand the homeless man said:

Give me a glass.
I will pour into it the water of a lake and I will hurl it
into the bottom of a volcano.
I will extinguish it
in the cone which burns without time.
Forever.

Give me a bottle.
I will seal a storm in it and I will pitch it to the bottom of
the sea.
There it will remain
in the oblivion of relics and lost pain.
For eternity.

Give me a barrel.
I will trap in it one hundred hurricanes and I will blast it
to the moon.
They will sweep its dark side,
in the desert where nobody will hear them howl.
Ever again.

Don't give me your fears.
You can keep them.
I have to finish my bottle,
count my pennies and read my book.
Each of these is more real that all your paranoias.

Today

Because
I can,
I deserve,
I need,
I want.
Because
it's not yesterday,
it's not tomorrow.
It's just today
and today is always
the perfect day.

The butterfly and the spider

I asked you to perceive the sudden breath of a caterpillar
as it transformed to a butterfly,
scared and lost in its web
waiting for a new day
that would come
after a lethargy
long and anxious,
enlarged with anguish and loneliness
uncertain through
pain and change.
In grey lament.

You preferred to stare at the constant glow in a spider's eyes
bold and defiant in its web
while waiting for a certain lunch.
Covetous
eager
yearning,
whatever the prey,
a cricket
a fly
or a mosquito.

The butterfly flew away.
The spider died in the web.
Of boredom.

A lapse of memory

In a lapse of memory
I found myself

staring into an unknown mirror:
a forgotten face
an unlearned name
an unnoticed scar
an unfelt pain
a not launched slap

a gun I've never had.

In a lapse of memory
I found myself

accosting, in involuntary acts:
lips to a love
a glass to a bottle
a sigh to a passion
a sleep to a numbness
a smile to a pain

a gun to my heart.

In a lapse of memory
I found myself.

I shot.

Song in the game of souls

Smoke is exhaled by a candle
abandoned in the playroom
of a sunken ship
between a forgotten past
a not found treasure
and a timeless present
cyclical in its senses.

The band of aching souls
plays chains like strings of a violin
and toasts with glasses emptied of wine.

Roulette spins ceaselessly,
the croupier throws the ball
then sees a shadow coming close.

The Joker outbid at Black Jack
splits and calls a card
invoking an ace never held.

Emaciated dancers kick the can can
in tattered clothes
grey as their rebellious days.

There are those who show the clock dreaming of divorce
those who hide a wedding ring while enjoying a whore
those who steal deftly in an open grave

The captain Cobra gets drunk
screams that the wind is back
blowing from the deep blue.

But the dance continues breathless
as the clock runs out of time
on the wall of a no sense world.

When the candle flame is extinguished
a curtain falls on the room.
Only wax remains.

Hyde Park dreaming

I was walking in the park
listening to the wind
singing among indifferent trees
looking at the gushing fountain
that spits at workers and tourists.

I saw an orchestra conductor directing nervous honking
at an intersection
while clouds of smoke enveloped the road.

I saw the white horse that jumps on the park chess board
eat his queen
and fly away, clasping the black bishop.

I saw the minotaur run from the fountain to the bell tower of Saint Mary
injuring his head as he knocked at the church door.

I saw an alcoholic drain a bottle and stand up to offer a flower
to a wounded woman, dragging her despair on heels.

I saw the tears of a caterpillar, forced against the wall of a dark chrysalis
squirming, desperate. It didn't want to become a butterfly.

I saw ...
No.
I turned around,
I looked for you
You weren't there.
I left.

Nessy

Dragged into a latent flaw
life after life
he found Nessy in a lake of thoughts
closed in a maze of madness,
tied like a dog
on a leash of disinherited battalions.

She watched the velvety dew
flood into the catacombs
of perfume sellers
while flocks of birds
circled in a sky
stained with blood.

The planet's faint glow dispersed
into shining starlight
but stars fell and burned.
Struck by lightning
eating up the land
like a shower of fire.

The wind blew away the dew
ululating like a herd of wolves.
Then the sky shut down.
Night came.
Nessy vanished.
It was dark.

Ghosts and a gun

Shoot!
Hungry ghosts
living in the limbo
of Samsara
during circus time.

Shoot!
A ghosts walks among no dead
and those who do not breathe
obsessed with what wasn't found
when the hands of gold gleamed.

Shoot!
Those ghosts who loved you
transforming blood into absinthe
shedding tears of incense,
burning flames of no sense.

Shoot!
Avid ghosts didn't wait
when lights covered you from the darkness
planting seeds of pain,
speaking of love.

Shoot!
Pious ghosts now smile
for masters disguised
as queens of the night
accepting coins of words.

Shoot!
Ghosts:
her, you, me.
Shoot ... shoot ...

A seagull

I loved you,
so keenly
to believe in you,
so deeply
to see you,
so madly
to hear you,
so foolishly
to follow you
in the beating of a seagull's wings
in his shrill tune
gliding on a current
defying gravity
oblivious of the people
of the stormy sea
of the sun.
You closed the window.

You in a thought

You, in a thought
elusive as love
intense as pain
then only memory,
the director of sick dreams,
never leaving
never caring
always biding time
like a mantis in a spider web
spun with obsessive pleasures.

A nightmare locked on your face
that I cannot caress
or forget,
a living phobia
in the anxious singing of cicadas,
drowned out by the roar of a raging sea.

The sea of love

You followed me
trampling footprints in the sand of my past.
You loved me
watching the wave that swept the shoreline of our present.
You left me
slipping between the mist that creeps into the night of existence.
I held you
immobilised in rocks like an anchor lost in memories.
I waited for you
chasing the foam that retreats in the backwash of another life.
I lost myself
drowned in the current that pushed me toward deep loneliness.

The forgotten beach

On the beach where waves carry
the sound of kids
with the screeching of seagulls
along the smile of their years not yet lived
in the shape of the salty foam that breaks onto rocks;
the freedom of their dreams
with the sand washed up by the white froth;
the hope of the unknown sucked into an undertow;
a storm that drags dreams, future and love
into a vortex of indifference.
There
on that beach
I have seen the birth of a flower
I call tomorrow.

Lost in the abyss

He said hello
he has taken the step
I know, I saw him
I met him
he talked to me
I was alone
I was walking in the streets of imprisoned madonnas,
supplicants
through the windows
closed for the evening
lit with candles,
as in forgotten cemeteries
where there's more beer than prayer
where ghosts circle
like drunks on a ship
in a stormy sea
thinking of the smiling bartender
who pours out desire,
distills jealousy,
empties the bottle.
There, in dew's infusion
torn petals fall
uprooted by edgy tears,
by suffering words
tenebrous
like the sea at night
where he lost his mind.
Into the abyss he entered,
he swam,
and from that lost land has returned.

The oblivion of the forgotten

A chain of words that run
faster than thought,
more useless than dreams,
more real than desires.

Fears on pastel-coloured signs.
The anxiety of a child
the suffering.

Then his path
a dull journey
as his hope is shipwrecked
among the waves of indifference
in a common sea
in a statistic
in the oblivion of the forgotten.

The voice of the universe

Red tears,
real tears,
dripped down the tombstone
of that dreamer
who believed
he saw the stars
in the lanterns on the lake
between net and fish
clouds and foolery
in a hazy dream
a hidden legend
as far away as waves
found in outer space
apparently with no sense
but the voice of the universe.

The missing moon

When the moon turned away at night,
she took everything,
even my dreams.
Illusions and hopes followed them
pulling the leash of a bewilderment,
where I still live without you.

Jupiter and Venus

Among the Milky Way's glittering sheets
Jupiter meets Venus –
an impulse, a glare
and in the sky they appear as two stars
close and shining.
So close it seems they are touching.
So shiny it seems they are reflecting.
So close it seems they are making love.
So shiny it seems they have already.

Andromeda's revenge

On a planetary stage
Medusa
with snakes chanting
sings the song of life
Perseo flees
desperate
Cetus hides
frightened
Cassiopeia leaves
for another galaxy.
The moon amused
dances
in deafening silence
watching the waves.
Andromeda breaks her chains,
ready
for her revenge.

Chaos

Looking into my eyes
you saw my soul.
In a black hole
and in that dark night
you were the only light.

You found my life
through a lot of lives.
Jumped in time
to the echo of desperate voices
to the jingle of abandoned glasses.

You saw a dancing star
in the chaos of my mind.

Eclipse

It was night and there were clouds.
He waited. In silence, he waited.

Timid stars broke through the dark cloak.
He walked. Slowly, he walked.

The moon rose, bright between the eyelids of the night.
He ran. Fast, he ran.

The eclipse began. All was dark.
He fell. Suddenly, he fell.

The night passed and the sun awoke.
He was dead. In one eclipse he was dead.

Supernova

A light dance in space:
your eyes,
your face
in the blood
of a star
as far away as a sun.

A shadow across a flag:
waving alone
cold in a volcano of moonstone
that burns
under a cloud of smoke.
No rain falls.

Me, you, ghosts
dead pirates lost,
darting flames
ice frozen in space,
a comet pierces the planet's face
a fire in a black lake.

Dark
look look look
Hot
run run run
Bang
scream scream scream.

It's a dream
as lived
on the lunatics path
in the loonies park
staring at the last
supernova star.

A night in a glass

Among the jarring notes of an aged jukebox
Among the smells of beer on the soaked floor
Among the voices of people lost
sitting in careless posture
Among forgotten smiles
as not given kisses
Among unfulfilled wishes
as not drunk drink
Among laughs synthesised by paid dreams
like sex wanted, not found and then bought
Among the forgotten memories of a life not lived
Among the faces of loved and then forgotten women
Among those wanted and never owned
or possessed and never had
I found a glass.
I looked into it
I saw the rum
I drank
I dreamed
I dallied.
It was mine
I was myself.

The silence of the wind

In silence
the wind blows
through the crowd.
Again

in a dome of noise
in a vacuum of voices
mixed in tone
in language
in coarse laughter
in tears dull
in eyes and on lips
in beer and spirits

in spontaneous happiness
as a new bottle
in distant memories
as one never finished
in known words
as one already drunk
in deep pain
as a filled glass.

In silence
the wind blows
through the crowd.
Always.

A dark pub

Looking for the sun in a dark pub
damp, moist from spilled beer
for that uncried tear
for that dormant desire
for that never arrived day
for that passed instant
for that not lived moment
for that lost second
for that betrayed minute
for that passed day
for that unexpected tomorrow
for that not granted occasion
for that not required punishment
for that not understood award
for that hurting memory
for that endured work
for that poisoned word
for that never thrown arrow
for that never sent flower
for that consumed friendship
for that never found treasure
for that never paid account
for that already left woman
for that played game
for that always dressed suit
for that never bought car
for that ever offered ring
for that refused diamond
for that forgotten dream
for that never waded river
for that not played match

for that postponed meeting
for that skipped appointment
for that disregarded promise
for that waiting hope
for that stolen desire
for that unrequited terror
for that vacant boredom
for that enjoyed solitude
for that not wanted company
for that dreaded question
for that grown anxiety
for that bottle now empty.

For that regret.
For that pain.
For that love.
For that excuse.

Or just for another glass.

A glass fixation

On the marble table
when the last drop evaporated,
the glass was found alone
faux
dried
cold
matt.

In the shadow
of desires unable to fly,
hypothetical thoughts stillborn
stuck in amber
constricted in a bottle
half full on the bar.

Unforgettable Obsession

No, it's not me, it's they who return.
Always.
The memories
the dreams
the threads of a life never had
which become garbled more than the past.
I am there. I look at them. I live them
as if real.
Ghosts who take possession of my body
sucking my soul.

And you?
You ask me to speak, to talk, to tell …
I've thrown away a lot of words
enough words
to fill a concrete truck.

What do you want to hear now?
That I told you yes.
Yes.
I'm ready.
I want to speak, to talk, to tell.
No.
I'm tired. Too tired.
I just want to drink.
Alone.

Do not look for me.
You would not find me.
You would not find me
even if I turned the bottle upside down.

The last rose

A rose fell in a glass

floating on ice
surfing through rum
mingling with my thoughts.

Your form appears as a drawing
impalpable
as the flight of a bird
inconsistent
as a message in the sky
blurring.

The rum vanishes
like the rose.
I never bought you
but always wore for you
as a precious ring.

A rose fell in a glass

withered on ice
marinated in rum
drowned by illusion.

Red lanterns

Red lanterns dance in silence.
The wind blows
from the north,
a seagull rises in flight,
an opalescent image, yours.
A smile, a look.
Desire.
Again silence,
the wind,
a sandstorm.
The seagull disappears
between shavings of cloud.
My soul is there
between the grains.
Sand in the sand
intangible.
Red lanterns dance
in the silence.
The wind blows
dissolving my illusion.

Lights in the night

Then one night I met you
in the reflection of the houses,
whizzing fast
colouring the window of the bus.

I saw your smile
in the glare of headlights,
shining tears
of rain on
smog veiled glass.

I touched your lips
of salty damp
fogged eyesight
covering our
cold silence.

I heard your gasp
of pleasure
in the creak of a seat
jerked forward,
the driver braking hard.

I tasted your scent
in a sea of sweat
velvet
your skin stained by craving
like a damaged seat.

I savoured,
you felt,
you touched.
I saw you …

go away
indifferent,
distracted.

You disappeared
as the lights of the city
gave way to early morning.

Venus's Eyes

I was painting dreams on a canvas of beer
looking at Venus's face on the digital wall.
Observing the sea
in the universe of her eyes
I heard waves caress the water's edge
felt salt pinch the skin
saw the moon paint deep silver blues.
Blinded
I was lost
then drenched.
Finally I woke
and you, Venus, you were there
in front of me
as real as
the sea in the universe of your eyes.

I would tell you that

I would tell you that …
whisper it in the night
stare at you.

I would tell you that …
while you slept
on the other side of the bed.

I would tell you that …
while you were dreaming
just close to my breast

I would tell you that…
kissing your back
touching your skin.

I would tell you that …
during the night
in a gentle breeze.

I would tell you that
I love you.

The sky above us

Look at the sky tonight,
What a night!
Look at the stars,
serene and bright
shining upon us.
They seem to jest
laughing at me
laughing at you
laughing at us.
I know, you know.

On this night
that grabs, binds and vanishes
I'd ask you
but my time
flew away with the wind.
You won't answer
and maybe you don't know.
I know, you know

I'll wait for you,
You won't come,
you'll erase me,
but you'll remember.
Perhaps you'll laugh,
at me
at you
at us.
I know, you know

Look at the sky tonight.
What a night!
I'll caress it,
I'll kiss it.
You'll look mute,
you'll want me,
but you'll give up
and you'll go.
I know, you know.

Yet I'll look for you
again
because your eyes
are a mantle of stars
that burns in my heart.
Whoever does not see the sun
slowly dies —
your glow
is the flame of my pain.

Waiting for the rain

Anywhere. I'd recognise the golden cloud that brings
rain to a meadow of stems and maidenhair, cradled by a
salty breeze.

It arrives unexpectedly, like a tropical storm.
It rains shiny droplets, like the sun's rays on waves.

A storm of imaginary diamonds filling the ether, nights
of roses and silences.
Passions and fears.

Under a cloth-white horizon I'm eyeing the sky, looking
for the golden cloud.
Waiting for the rain.

Me and You

I'm in you,
you're in me
as water gives life
as the sun heats life.

Our souls wandered
in the dark space of time
to reach the shrine of a sparkling destiny.
Lives after lives
lies after lies.
Attracted to a gravitational joke
that knows no distance
nor any border it passes.

Moved by a perpetual motion,
together our souls will dance
into the zodiac's romance
accompanied by the planet's orchestra.
Between vaulting sparkling comets
we will live eternal moments.

At the end of time
found in sweet night
embracing us,
we'll fly
with silent stars
illuminated by
an endless flame:
our love.

Night road to life

It's night. Well, for me it's always been a little 'night'. Even at noon. Even in summer, when the sun whips the breakwater rocks that protect the beach from an angry sea. Angry, hitting back against the brutal, careless intrusion of men.

Even then. Even now. The night is a cloak that covers not only the sky. It envelops the earth, trees, rivers, or the dead, ready for burial.

The night envelops souls.

And my soul has never done anything to throw off its dark shroud.

I drink. Well, I have always drunk a bit. Even when I had company. As friends we would run about laughing, joking, lending a serious tone to a jumble of illusions. Sandy ridges landsliding in torrential rain.

Even then. Even now. The bottle is a vessel that contains not only alcohol, water, fruit juice or urine for analysis.

The bottle contains souls.

And my soul has never done anything to find the exit from its labyrinth of mirrors.

I'm on the road. Well, I have always been partly on the road. Even when I had a house. A family. When there were parties, dinners and singing under one roof, lit by smiles or doubts.
Even then. Even now. The road runs not only for cars, for goods or for animals going to slaughter.

The road runs for souls.

And my soul has never done anything to hate the loneliness of asphalt.

It has travelled with a selfish and obsessive love. Possessive love. To the limit. Until the road has reached summer, friends, home, family.

Life itself.

From the same author

L'uomo che salvò il mondo (The man who saved the world)

L'uomo che salvò il mondo (The man who saved the world) is published in Italy by Lettere Animate editore. In his first novel, Ferdinando Manzo tells a post-apocalyptic story which takes place in a new world where survivors live divided between three cities: white, black and yellow, according to their race. The main character leaves his city with a mission to save the world. So begins an odyssey in which different destine are woven together. There are stories of unhappy and loneliness, with some twists. A sci-fi thriller outlining the final days of humanity.

Category: FICTION THRILLER/SCI-FI/POST-APOCALYPTIC

ARCO:
the legend of the blue vortex

An exciting new story from first-time novelist, Ferdinando Manzo, Arco explores man's battle with the sea in an attempt to seek solace.
The story is set in two different eras: on the high seas among ancient pirates and in contemporary Europe ravaged by war. The legend of the blue vortex – a door into another world – is the central focus of both periods.
An adventure story, it also raises philosophical questions about love and the purpose of life.

Category: FICTION MAGICAL REALISM/ROMANCE/FANTASY

From the same publisher

Angela's anorexia: the story of my mother

A son's story of the debilitating illness, anorexia nervosa, that his single mother suffered from throughout his childhood. The mother and son formed a close bond and the boy's description of their life together is filled with both joy and sadness. A true story showing the boy's experience of growing up fast in Australia and New Zealand, caring for his mother while coming to understand her sickness and his need to develop an independent spirit early on.

Damian Cooper has written a straightforward, honest and loving account of his boyhood, set against a poignant parallel story of his mother's excessive focus on body image, food, diet and exercise.

Category: SELF-HELP/EATING DISORDERS AND BODY IMAGE

Burma my mother And Why I Had to Leave

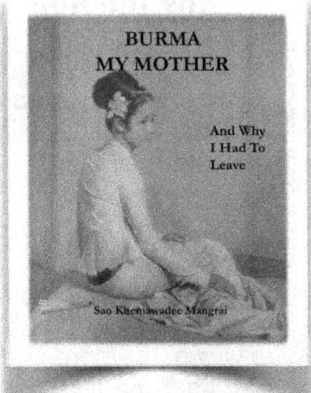

Myanmar's future is informed by its past - and BURMA MY MOTHER tells it like it is.
A valuable story of living through good times and plenty of bad in Burma, now known as Myanmar, before an escape to a new life of freedom.

Author **Sao Khemawadee Mangrai**'s husband, Hom, was imprisoned for 5 years, and his father was shot and killed sitting alongside independence leader, General Aung San, when he was assassinated.

Khemawadee grew up in a Shan state in the north-east of Myanmar, previously known as Burma, and now lives in Sydney. Her sad memories are also infused by the beauty of the country and the grace of Myanmar's Buddhist culture.

Category: MEMOIR

Drenched by the Sun

**I, who prophesy
by reading the stars
and the wind,
now think of that
country ...**

Syam Sudhakar 'has an eye for the strange and the uncanny and a way of building translucent metaphors,' according to leading South Indian poet, K. Satchidanandan.

An award-winning poet who writes in English and Malayalam, Sudhakar is based in Kerala, teaching and researching Indian poetry.

Category: POEMS

Road to Rishi Konda

'Road to Rishi Konda' by **Geetha Waters** is a memoir of insight and charm, with a serious educational purpose. The author recalls delightful and stimulating stories from her childhood to throw light on the work of the philosopher J. Krishnamurti as a revolutionary 20th century educator.

At once fascinating and enchanting, Geetha Waters' stories centre on a girl growing up in Kerala and Andhra Pradesh in the '60s and '70s.

These youthful tales are underpinned by Geetha's deep understanding of childhood education, based both on her academic studies and in practice in her daily life as a mother and childcare professional. Written from a child's perspective, the tales of awakening to life offer the reader an opportunity to appreciate how all children learn, as they draw on a deep well of curiosity that needs to be respected.

Category: MEMOIR/BURMA-HISTORY

Road to Mandalay Less Travelled

'The Road to Mandalay Less Travelled' by **Ingrid Raj** provides research on a selection of Anglo-Burmese writing published from the period of British rule up in Burma up until 2007. What Raj shares with us in this study is the knowledge she gained about the value of social resistance achieved through writing. Both fiction and non-fiction texts are included in arguing a case that these might be viewed as tools of often ambivalent resistance against oppressive regimes, both local and colonial. Her research deserves a wider readership than was initially provided, and to this aim Sydney School of Arts & Humanities presents the work as its first publication in this new category of Essays & Theses. We hope that specialist researchers as well as members of the general reading public take this opportunity to learn more about the culture of the people of Myanmar through their unique approach to storytelling, based largely on their religious understanding, their rich store of folk legend and their chequered history.

Category: MEMOIR/LITERATURE/BURMA-HISTORY

Jiddu Krishnamurti World Philosopher Revised Edition

The life of the 20th-century philosopher Jiddu Krishnamurti was truly astonishing. As this new updated edition shows, people from all over the world would gather to hear him speak the wisdom of the ages.

Biographer **Christine (CV) Williams** carried out research over a period of four years to write this ebook account of Krishnamurti's life. She studied his major archive of personal correspondence and talks, and interviewed people who knew him intimately.

Krishna was born into poverty in a South Indian village, before being adopted by a wealthy English public figure, Annie Besant. As an adult he settled in California, travelling to India and England every year to give public lectures that inspired spiritual seekers beyond any single religion.

Category: BIOGRAPHY

www.ingramcontent.com/pod-product-compliance
Lightning Source LLC
LaVergne TN
LVHW041457070426
835507LV00009B/650